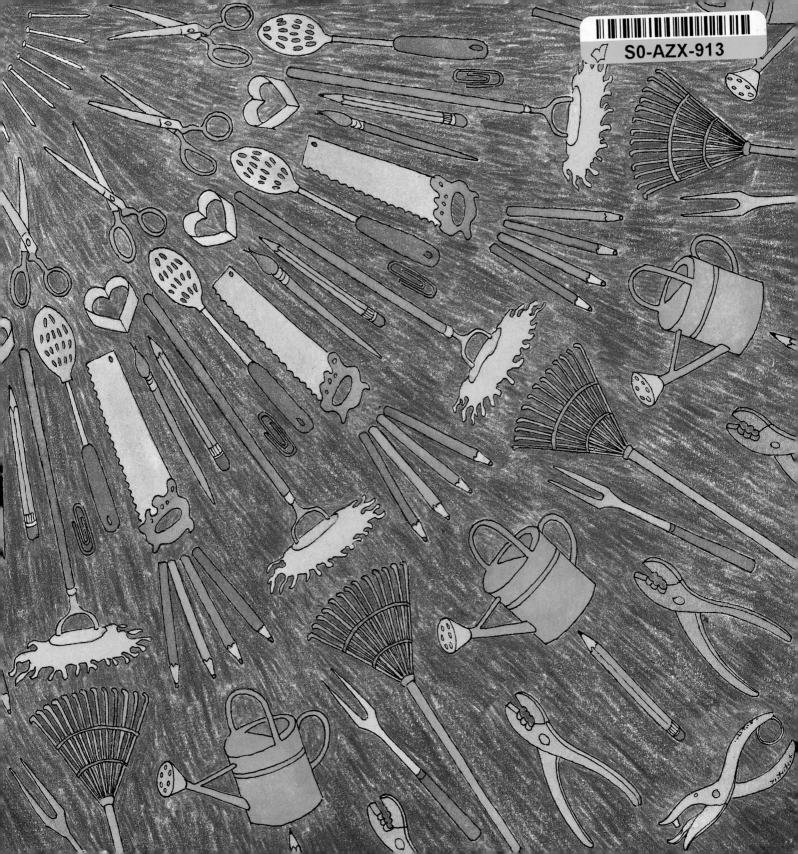

To Isabel
and
Elizabeth

Published by Crown Publishers, Inc., a Random House company, 201 East 50th Street, New York, New York 10022
CROWN is a trademark of Crown Publishers, Inc.

Manufactured in Italy

Library of Congress Cataloging-in-Publication Data
Kelley, True.
Hammers and mops, pencils and pots / by True Kelley.
p. cm.
Summary: Labeled illustrations present various kinds of tools and implements used in the kitchen, in the garden, in art class,
at the office, and in other settings.1. Implements, utensils, etc. — Juvenile literature.
2. Tools—Juvenile literature. [1. Implements, utensils, etc. 2. Tools. 3. Vocabulary.]
I. Title.
TX298. K43   1994
683.8—dc20   93-25294
ISBN 0-517-59626-1

10 9 8 7 6 5 4 3 2 1   First Edition

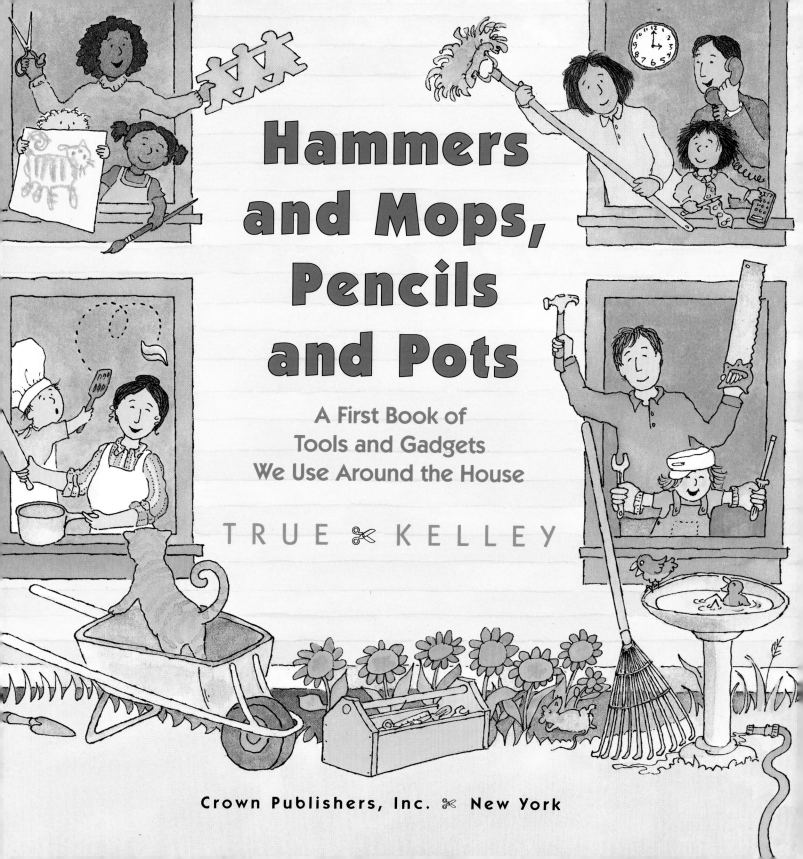

Hammers and Mops, Pencils and Pots

A First Book of Tools and Gadgets We Use Around the House

TRUE ✂ KELLEY

Crown Publishers, Inc. ✂ New York

Out in the Garden

sun hat

garden gloves

worm

boots

spade

shovel

garden fork

hoe

edger

trowel

hand cultivator

pruning shears

pruning saw

bulb planter

garden cart

lawnmower

leaf rake

seedling tray

flowerpots

hedge clippers

packet of seeds

lopping shears

garden rake

birdbath

scarecrow

wheelbarrow

tiller

sprinkler

garden hose

watering can

Rake, Hoe, Shovel, Grow!

In the Workshop

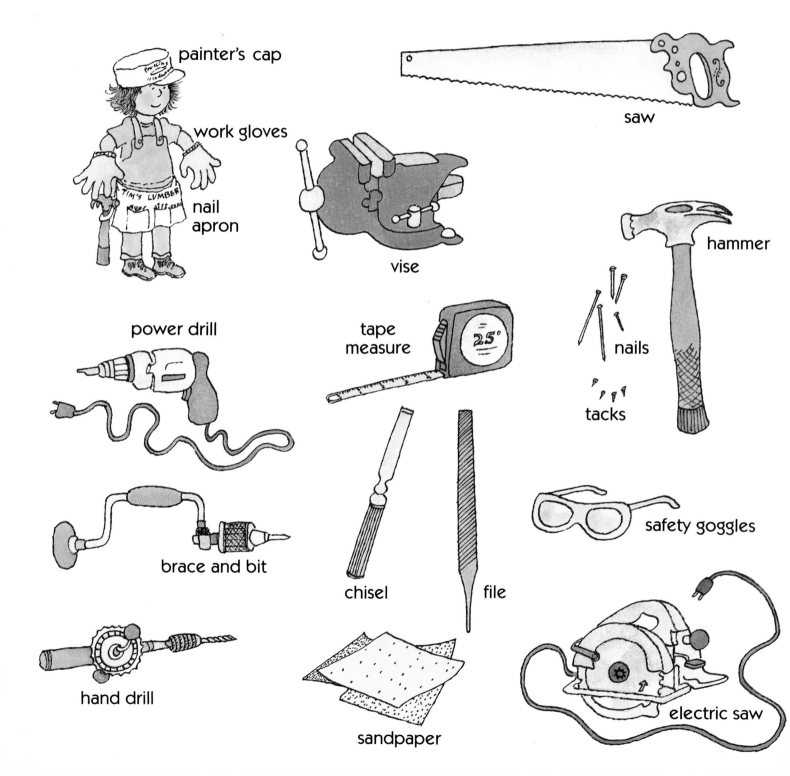

painter's cap

work gloves

nail apron

saw

vise

hammer

nails

tacks

power drill

tape measure

brace and bit

chisel

file

safety goggles

hand drill

sandpaper

electric saw

square
nut

wing
nut

hex
nut

bolt

screw

pliers

screwdriver

Phillips screwdriver

stepladder

wire cutters

C-clamp

paint roller and tray

paintbrushes

wrench

adjustable wrench

plane

paint pail

sawhorse

level

Hammer, Nails, Pliers, Pails!

In the Art Room

self-portrait

scissors

smock

chalk

CHALK
CHALK

blackboard

marker pens

colored pencils

PAINT

RED

BLUE

poster paints

fingerpaints

CRAYONS

crayons

template

ART PAPER

paper

paper pad

palette

ruler

glue

glitter

easel

tape

yarn

watercolor set

modeling clay

paintbrushes

pipe cleaners

modeling dough

ink

ink pen

eraser

paint tube

pencil

pencil sharpener

Paper, Clay, Paints, Play!

In the Kitchen

chef's hat

muffin tin

pie pan

salt and pepper shakers

brownie pan

potholder

cake pan

apron

cookie sheet

measuring cup

blender

cookbook

rolling pin

spatula

slotted spoon

forks

whisk

mixing spoon

wooden spoon

ice cream scoop

potato masher

corkscrew

scoop

measuring spoons

funnel

ladle

timer

mug

glasses

cup and saucer

bowl

plate

pot

grater

colander

pitcher

skillet

pizza cutter

beaters

wok

cleaver

paring knife

steamer

bread knife

cutting board

potato peeler

juicer

teakettle

can openers

cookie cutters

teapot

Pots, Beaters, Pans, Eaters!

In the Office

briefcase

clock

one-hole punch

scissors

calculator

pushpin

tack

eraser

pencil

paper clip

ballpoint pen

wastebasket

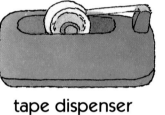
tape dispenser

stapler

dictionary

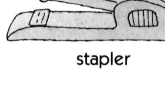
bulldog clip

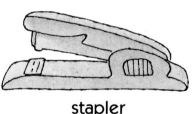
rubber bands

stamp pad

rubber stamp

computer

office chair

typewriter

pencil sharpener

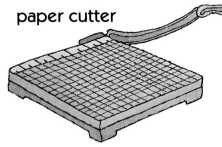
paper cutter

stamps

file folder

paper

rotary file

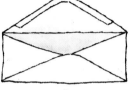
envelope

tape

file cabinet

telephone answering machine

desk

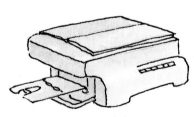
copy machine

fax machine

address book

memo pad

mug

appointment calendar

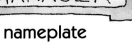
MANAGER
nameplate

Computer, Paper, Pens, Stapler!

Time to Clean!

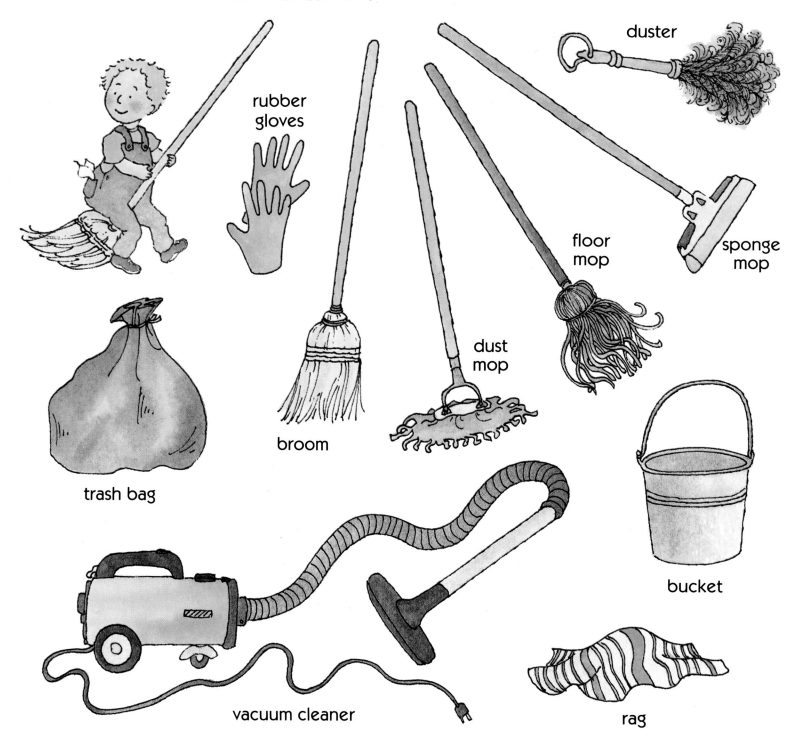

rubber gloves

duster

floor mop

sponge mop

dust mop

trash bag

broom

bucket

vacuum cleaner

rag

clothespin

laundry basket

washer

dryer

dustpan

hanger

sponge

brush

toothbrush

vegetable brush

bottles

Cans

wastebaskets

WINDOW CLEANER

sprayer

BLAST
Laundry Soap

Dish Soap

CLEANSER

soap

dish towel

paper towels

Mop, Vacuum, Duster, Broom!

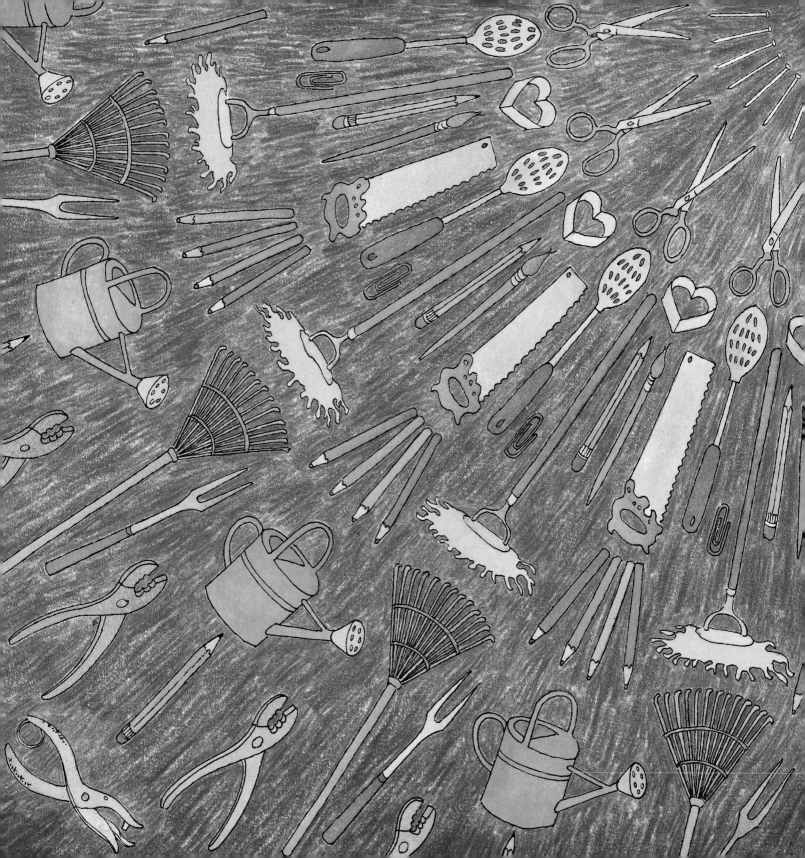